Dogmas:
Secrets to loving your Dog

Other RJLA, Inc. Books

Dogmas:
Secrets to loving your Dog.

Written by: Robert Uherka & Lauren Scott
With Illustrations by: Margarita Bartling

RJLA, Inc.
ISBN # 1-891194-01-1

Inquiries and excerpt requests should be addressed to:
RJLA, Inc.
P.O. Box 467831
Atlanta, GA 31146
ISBN # 1-891194-01-1

With love to our
boisterous pack;
Bailey, Taylor, Corky
and Bomber.

Begin each day
by *Greeting*
your *dog*
with a
HELLO
and **HUG.**

Take him to the pet store and let him PICK out a NEW toy.

Schedule

daily *exercise* &
PLAYTIME, this is
your time to **BOND**,
relax, & have
FUN with your dog.

Encourage

your *dog* to

EXPLORE

outdoor areas...

..where you've **hidden**

his **favorite**

TREATS

for him to find.

Bring **TREATS** for your *dogs* on all **outings** and be willing to **share** with other **HUNGRY** canines.

Take your dog

swimming.

Don't forget the sunscreen!

Bring grooming **tools** to the PARK with you and your *dog...*

..and **take** time
during your outing
to *relax* and
GROOM him.

Find **GAMES**

to engage

your *dog's*

natural

inclination...

..of **HERDING,**

tracking,

or **HUNTING.**

For **single** *dogs,* adopt a **pal** for him.

Many *dogs*
can be very lonely
by **themselves.**

Sign up

for an

OBEDIENCE

class or a

BRUSH-UP class.

Teach your dog
a **TRICK** and
encourage him
to **show**
everyone
his new talent.

Make a Date

with your dog

to do his *favorite*

ACTIVITIES.

Plan a **double** *Date* with a **friend** and their *dog.*

When possible,

include

your *dog*

in your

OUTINGS &

errands.

Give your *dog* a PAW massage.

Take your *dog* **camping**, don't forget to **bring** his **bed** or mat to lay on.

Find
your *dog*
a playmate.

Purchase a **stuffed** animal

companion

for your *dog.*

Many *dogs* will **adopt them** **carry** them around without destroying them.

Leave a
radio or **TV** on

when you are away from
HOME...

..the **SOUNDS** will help **soothe** your **pet.**

Provide interesting

outdoor **VIEWS**

by leaving your

curtains OPEN

so your *dog* can

look OUTSIDE.

If windows are **HIGH**,

place a

box or **STOOL**

nearby to help

your dog **REACH**

his window **view.**

Take your dog to **WORK.** He'll be *fascinated* with your office and will **love** to help you with any *special* deliveries

Regularly **clean** your *dog's* sleeping area (blankets, pillows, beds).

Take your 4-legged friend to *dog*-related **events** like dog **walk-a-thons.**

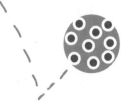

Hire a *dog* *walker* for days when **you can't** be there.

Discover an *exercise* that you and your dog can both **ENJOY.**

Remember to do an *easy* warm up and **cool** down during **pet** **exercise** sessions.

Develop a *routine* with your *dog*, to do the **ACTIVITY** the same time **every** day.

(Dogs love routine)

Ask someone to fill-in for you when you can't be there for your routine. A pet day care center may be an alternative as well.

On **nice** days,

open the

windows

to let in the

outdoor **smells**

& SOUNDS.

Phone **HOME** & leave *messages* for your *dog.*

Plan **quiet time**

with your *dog*

to sit and **ENJOY** his

companionship.

Take time to **learn** your *dog's* language.......

what's he really *trying* to tell you???

Get involved,

join a *dog*

CLUB.

Invest in an

ID tag

for your *dog.*

LAUGH

with your dog,

tell him

a **joke.**

Sing a song to your *dog*,

who knows,

maybe your dog will

singalong.

Take **lots**
of **pHOTOs**
of your **DOG.**

Capture him
sleeping,
playing,
hunting...

Include *your dog* *in* **family** photos *and* videos.

For **active** dogs, take him for a **jog.**

Take
your *dog*
on a **leisurely**
walk...

..and let

him **smell**

the *flowers*

along the way.

TALK to your dog, **tell** him a **story** .....and, **listen** to his **stories.**

Take your dog

for rides in

the car.

Make up **NEW** games to play with your **DOG.**

Let him help you **unpack** your

shopping **bags,**

he'll love the

sights and

smells.

Take your *dog* to
visit elderly or
children.

Buy or rent a

VIDEO

made *for*

DOGS.

Train your dog to **sit** politely when **GREETING** Visitors.

Invite a neighbor's or friend's **DOG** over for a day of **play.**

For **WORKING** **parents,** check out local *dog* **daycare...**

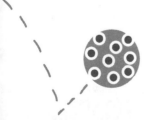

..to **leave your** *dog* while you're at **WORK.**

Take your dog **out** to *eat* and let him *people* **watch...**

..don't forget to *bring* a rawhide chew **bone** or **TOY** along with a *water* **bowl.**

Let your **DOG** lead you on a **nature** **HIKE.**

Encourage
your **DOG** to **use**

his **nose...**

..create a **track** for him to **sNIFF** out by placing his favorite **treats** along the **PATH...**

..as a *Special* reward, put his favorite **toy** at the **END** of the **trail.**

Be sure to

take **fresh** water

for your **DOG**

on **all** your

OUTINGS.

Buy a **bOOK** with *dog* treat **ReCiPeS** and bake some on a **raiN**y **day.**

Teach your DOG to FETCH...

...*frisbees*, **balls**, *or newspapers.*

Create

a backyard play-ground.

Put in a
sandBOX
and hide his
favorite **TOYS**
in the sand.

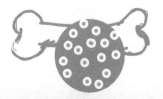

Hang

a sturdy

toy

from a tree for him **to**

TUG on.

Ramps and **HURDLES**

in the backyard can prepare

your **DOG**

for agility.

A **LARGE** *Dog* may enjoy an *old* **tire**

to **chew**,
TUG, *or*
chase.
(avoid steel belt tires)

Coordinate

a dog PLAY

group that

meets on a

regular basis.

Play **hide & SEEK** in the house or outside. Dogs **love** to **sNIFF** out their owners.

Buy chew toys designed to keep dogs' TEETH clean.

Clean **TEETH** mean *fresher* breath.

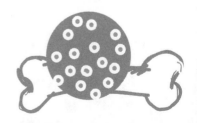

Buy mint **flavored** tennis **balls** to give him *minty* breath.

Take your
DOG on a
bike trip.

(Peddle at his speed)

Outfit your

dog with **PAW**

protectors...

(doggie booties)

..if you and

your dog **HIKE**

on **rough** terrain

or in **severe**

cold or

heat.

PROTECT
your *dog* from
the cold...

..by investing in a *doggy* **jacket** for those long **treks** in the **winter** months.

For **LARGE** dogs, **older** dogs or dogs with **injuries**,

raise their food and water **bowls** so they don't have to **bend** over to eat or drink.

Be sure your **DOG** has a **soft**, dry sleeping area.

His **sleeping** area should be **COOL** in the summer and **WARM** in the winter.

Replace or
re-stuff your dog's bed or
pillow once they lose their
fluffiness.

Hide TREATS in the house for your *dog* *to find.*

Sit **quietly**

with your pet and

enjoy his

PRESENCE.

If he's not allowed on the **furniture**, then sit on the floor with him. Dogs **LOVE** to **lay** next to their friends.

If you can't take your **dog** with you on an excursion, then **bring** home SOUVENIRS for him to **smell...**

..like sticks,
grass, *leaves*,
or **ROCKS.**
They love to do that for us!

Try **natural** healthy treats. Many dogs love **carrots**, *apples* and other FRESH produce. No dip required.

Buy a **membership** to a **biscuit** of the month **CLUB.**

Indulge

your dog with

a special **TREAT**

with a **teeny bit**

of leftover

fish or **MEAT.**

Just remember,

too much of a

good thing

may make your DOG

fat.

Tie a **ball**
or **stuffed** sock
on a rope and

attach it to a **pole**...

...Many dogs loveto **jump** and **chase** this while you *swing it* around.

Regularly *practice*

obedience

lessons.

Personalize *your* **DOG's COLLAR.**

Leave only a *few* **dog TOYS** out at a time and place the remaining toys in a *Special* **basket** or **Box.**

Switch them out regularly so he doesn't get **bored** with any one toy. Only allow a *few* **TOYS** out a time.

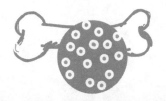

Cut a hole
in your fence
so your dog
can look out
and SEE
beyond the yard...

...He'll be **less BORED** and keep an *eye* on the **neighborhood.**

To give your **arm**
a break and a chance
for your *DOG* to
run further...

..use a tennis racket to **send** balls flying for your *DOG* to **retrieve.**

Enter your

DOG

in a

CONTEST...

..most **SPOTS**,
smallest dog,
BIGGEST dog,
best dog *trick*...

To add **INTEREST**
to an **old toy**,
try rubbing a little

peanut butter

or soft

cheese on it.

Take your **DOG** to a local ice cream shop for a **baby** ice cream **CONE.**

Buy a **ReFLeCTiVe** collar or bandana so **CARS** and *people* can see him at *night.*

Teach your **DOG**

to *catch*

a Frisbee.

(many dogs prefer soft ones)

Give *your* dog a **massage** .

Begin with his **HEAD** and work toward his **tail**.

Enter your **DOG** in an **owner/dog** look alike **CONTEST.**

Remember to **pack** your dog's favorite *toy* and **BED** on any *overnight* stays.

Schedule plenty of **outdoor** time for you indoor dog.

Even just **Sitting** outside

on a leash **under** a

TREE can be

ENTERTAINING.

Introduce your dog **to everyone** and **include** him in *social* activities at home.

When possible,

take your

dog

to a

PARTY!

Remember
your *dog*
on **HOLIDAYS**
and birthdays.

He'll **love** the extra

attention

and gifts.

Purchase an **outdoor** water sprinkler or wading **pool...**

..your *dog* may love to **play** in it during those **HOT** **summer** days.

Dance
with your DOG!

He'll probably

prefer a

slow Dance.

Keep your dog in **tip-top** shape. Be sure he's **current** on all his **vaccinations** **& checkups**

Go ahead,

BARK,

yip

or **HOWL**

with your **DOG.**

Include your **DOG** in your **camping** trips .... and don't forget his **pup-tent!**

For **CAR** travel,

keep a *dog*

travel kit

in your car...

..that includes

fresh **water**,

water **bowl**,

first aid kit,

and a towel.

Travel
Kit

Compliment
your **DOG**,
tell him all about his
Special
qualities
that you love...

...Maybe he's

handsome,

adorable,

wonderful,

Lovable,

SILLY,

sensitive...

End

each day with a warm,

FURRY goodnight

hug.